For my Secret Santa

© 2021, The Christmas Eve Visitor

 G&G Pub House

Kathryn Gilbreath, Author & Illustrator

All rights reserved. No part of this publication may be reproduced, distributed, or transmitted in any form by any means, including photocopying, recording, or other electronic methods without the prior written permission of the author, except in the case of brief quotations embodied in reviews and certain other noncommercial uses permitted by copyright law. For permission requests, email the editor at email address listed below.

G&G Pub House
attn: Kathryn Gilbreath
GGPubHouse@gmail.com

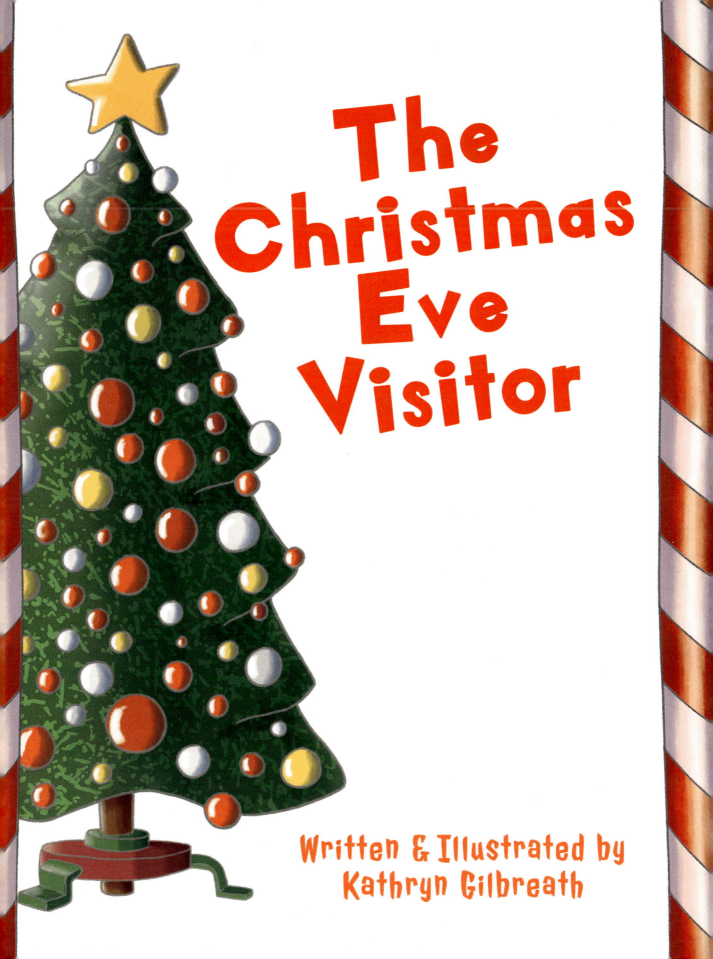

It was Christmas Eve and my family was sleeping
No TVs, no cell phones, nothing was beeping.

Our tree was bedecked with a star on the top;
With high hopes that Santa would make a quick stop.

The kids were all tucked in their beds nice and neat,
While dreaming of all the sweet treats they'd eat.

I was startled awake, my eyes opened wide,
I heard the jingling of bells from somewhere outside!

Jingle
Jingle
Jingle

I ran to the window and stuck out my head,
It was cold. It was dark. I missed my warm bed.

The moon was so bright it lit up the night skies,
Yet still, I had trouble believing my eyes
As I looked upon an incredible sight
Of a sleigh with nine reindeer circling in flight!

The sleigh's skillful driver, and this is no joke,
Looked just like the guy in those ads selling Coke!
His reindeer were fast like a missile in flight;
So fast that the driver was holding on tight.

"Whoa Dasher! Slow Dancer! Easy now, Vixen!
Down Comet! Halt Cupid. This rooftop here, Blitzen!
Prancer and Donner, please stay on your toes!
And Rudolph, remember to dim that red nose!"

Carefully steering his fantastical sled, Santa guided the Reindeer right over my head! He landed the sleigh with a jangling noise, Then reached in the back for his sack full of toys.

Before I could wonder
"Hey! Where did he go?"
I heard someone laugh
with a loud "Ho Ho Ho!"
"Could it be that Santa
was now in my house?"
"Oh what should I do?
Should I wake up my spouse?"

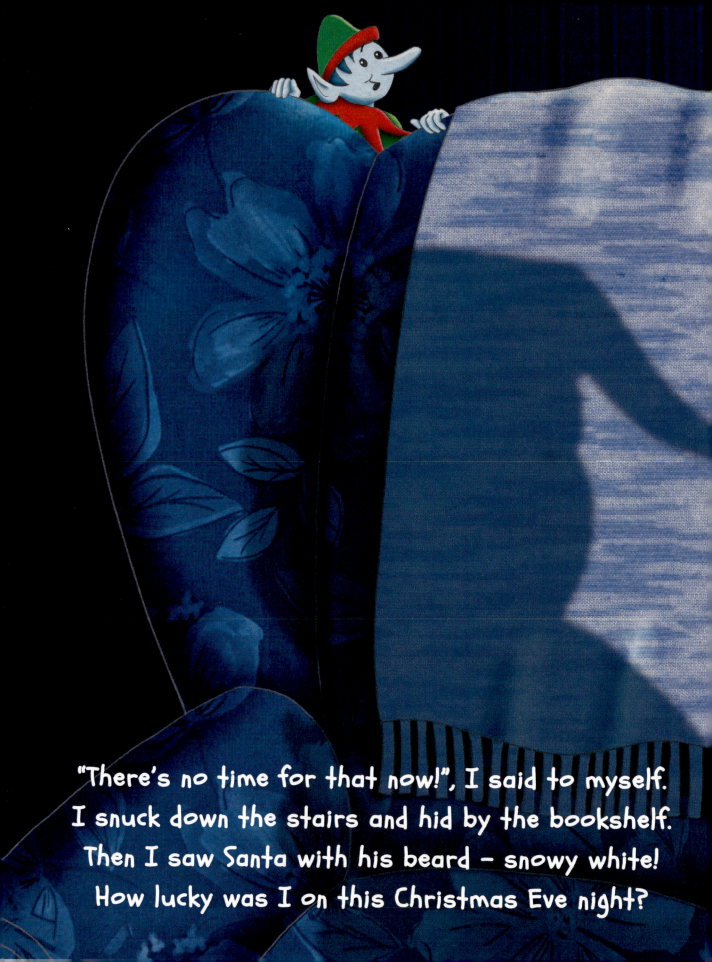

"There's no time for that now!", I said to myself.
I snuck down the stairs and hid by the bookshelf.
Then I saw Santa with his beard – snowy white!
How lucky was I on this Christmas Eve night?

He wore a red suit
with a wide, white fur trim
A pointed red hat
with more fur 'round the rim.
He wasn't as plump
as in all of his pics,
Like he ate less cookies
and more carrot sticks!

He seemed really friendly;
a right jolly old elf,
Much bigger than the one
sitting up on my shelf.
Although he was broad
and rather quite hairy,
His smile was so warm,
he was not at all scary.

He opened his pack, filled with presents galore, Placed them 'neath the tree; nearly covering the floor.

And when he was done,
gave a tug on his beard,
Then, in a flash,
Santa Claus disappeared!

Up on the rooftop
I heard jangling once more.
I ran 'cross the room
and dashed out of the door.
As Santa waved at me
'fore flying away,
I heard him exclaim
"Have a Great Christmas Day!"

Made in the USA
Middletown, DE
03 May 2021